THE MAYANS GAVE THEIR ART AND ARCHITECTURE

HISTORY 3RD GRADE

Children's History Books

BABY PROFESSOR

EDUCATION KIDS

Speedy Publishing LLC

40 E. Main St. #1156

Newark, DE 19711

www.speedypublishing.com

Copyright 2017

All Rights reserved. No part of this book may be reproduced or used in any way or form or by any means whether electronic or mechanical, this means that you cannot record or photocopy any material ideas or tips that are provided in this book

The Mayans created a powerful and complex civilization that lasted for over two thousand years in what is now Mexico and Central America. Let's look at what their art and buildings were like.

CHICHEN ITZA

MAYAN CULTURE

The Mayans created great cities all through their territory. They decorated their cities with statues, carvings, and pillars. The pillars were decorated, and were carved with stories about great kings and battles the Mayans won.

The Mayans worked hard to please their king, and, through him, to please the gods. A lot of their art, and of their important buildings, connected to how they prayed to the gods and tried to do would please them.

Palenque glyphs

MAYAN ART

One of the neat things about Mayan art is that the artists signed their work! This means historians can see the hand of the same artist in many carvings, murals, or other work. Mayan artists did not have metal tools or devices like a potter's wheel, but they still created amazing carvings, jewelry, and pottery.

ANCIENT MAYAN GRANITE TABLET

A lot of Mayan art is pictures of the gods and what they do, or gifts to be offered to the gods. There are also images of kings and armies, people doing everyday things like hunting or farming, animals,

MURALS

and plants. The animals and plants were not the important subjects, though; those were almost always the gods or the heroes and kings.

M ost Mayan statues, carvings, and murals had Mayan writing as well. The writing is very complex and beautiful, so you can think of

K1081

it as an art form in itself. Learn about it in the Baby Professor book *The Mayans' Calendars and Advanced Writing System*.

CANCUEN PANEL

A lot of the best Mayan art we have was created to honor great events, great people, or the gods. Most of the figures in the pictures and carvings seem to be real people, not characters made up by the artists.

At the ruins of the city of Copan is a stairway and series of ramps supported by statues of people and other carved figures. This is probably related to the ceremony when a new Mayan ruler became king.

City of Copan Ruins

TRIPOD VESSEL

POTTERY

On Mayan pottery, often there is a picture of the king sitting while important visitors come to see him. Sometimes the name of the king and his family are included. The clothing, face painting, and other details of what Mayans wore when they went to see the king are faithfully included. These details change over time, so pottery from different centuries shows different clothing styles.

Hats were important to the Mayans, and what kind of hat you could wear showed what your role was in the world! In the pottery and other carvings the subjects are often wearing hats. The hat of an important person might have big flowers and hummingbirds, or even a fish!

Mayan Mask Carvings

Along with vases and other objects that had pictures on their sides, Mayan artists also made many figures of people and animals. These were not toys.

Many of the examples we have were buried with important people, like kings, when they died. Explorers found the tombs in the last 150 years, and found the pottery figures inside.

SCULPTURE

The Mayans made many stand-alone works of art, often great carved stones. The carvings are often histories of a king or a royal family. Some of the carvings describe religious ceremonies, including sacrifices, and may have been set up near where the ceremony usually took place.

Maya Presentation of Captives

Mayan Jade

Some of the Mayan sculptures had inlays of jade for eyes or for decorations.

J ade is a very hard, dense, material, and it is amazing what the Mayans were able to do with it without having metal tools to help them.

PAINTINGS

Very few Mayan paintings have survived to today, because Central America is so humid that painted cloth wears out and decays quickly. However, some painted murals from around 100 CE have been found at San Bartolo. They show scenes from stories about the corn god, and are the oldest Mayan paintings we have yet found.

MAYAN PAINTINGS

MAYAN PYRAMID

MAYAN ARCHITECTURE

The Mayans built remarkable cities, often in places in mountainous jungle that must have been hard to get to. The cities had a regular series of features, but often grew irregularly beyond the city center. This is different from Aztec cities to the north, which were much more carefully laid out.

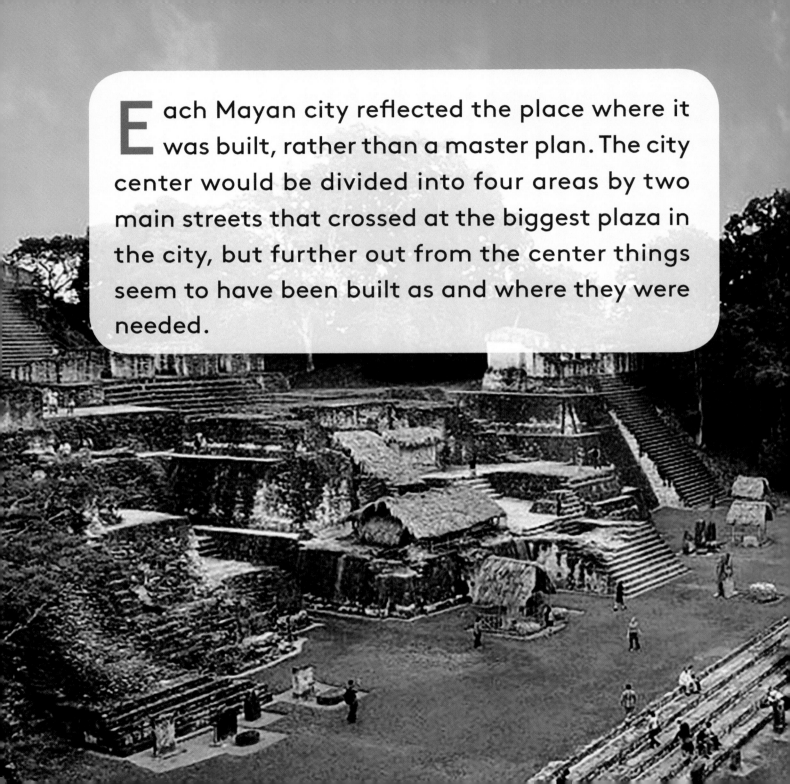

Each Mayan city reflected the place where it was built, rather than a master plan. The city center would be divided into four areas by two main streets that crossed at the biggest plaza in the city, but further out from the center things seem to have been built as and where they were needed.

Mayan Palenque

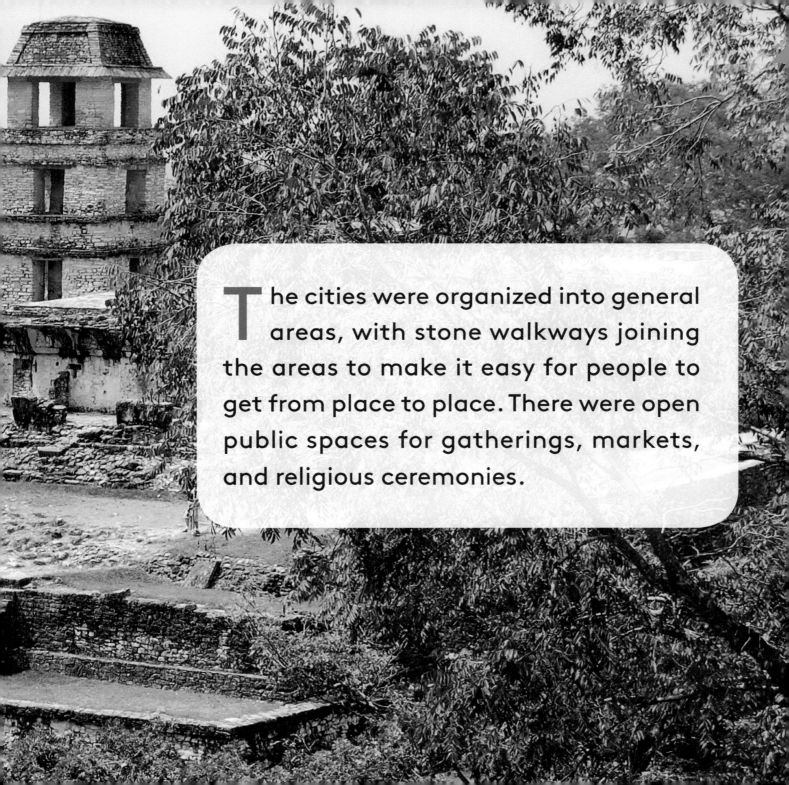

The cities were organized into general areas, with stone walkways joining the areas to make it easy for people to get from place to place. There were open public spaces for gatherings, markets, and religious ceremonies.

One big difference from early European cities is that Mayan cities usually did not have defensive walls or fortifications. Only in the sixteenth century, as the Mayan empire began to come apart, did some cities put up walls in attempt to slow down enemy attacks.

The Mayans did have a theory about making the central line of each city, from the pyramid of the main temple out to the far end of the main plaza, line up with a pattern of the stars and the Earth's orbit around the sun. In some ways, each city was a large observatory, especially for marking things like the summer solstice (when the sun is highest in the sky).

Most of the great buildings in a Mayan city were related to the gods, or to the king. Some buildings are also related to calendars, which Mayans found very important! There is a pyramid with four staircases, each one with 91 steps. All those steps, plus the flat area at the top of the pyramid, makes 365 "steps", in honor of the days of the year. The pyramid also has eighteen sections around the staircases, the number of the months in a Mayan year.

MAYAN PYRAMID

TEOTIHUACAN

PLATFORMS

◇◇◇◇◇◇◇◇◇◇◇◇◇◇◇◇◇◇

A city might have several platforms made of limestone, raised about ten feet in the air. People could gather around on the street below to see the ceremony or religious event that would happen there. The platforms often had decorations of ball players or of people involved in sacrifices to the gods.

PYRAMIDS AND TEMPLES

The key structure in a Mayan city are the pyramids at its center. Unlike Egyptian pyramids that have four smooth sides that come up to a point at the top, Mayan pyramids have several levels and staircases on their four sides, so they are sometimes called step-pyramids. At the top of the pyramid there would be a flat area, not a point, and on this flat area there was often a temple.

RUINS IN GUATEMALA

Each pyramid was in honor of one of the Mayan gods. Some of the pyramids were 200 feet high, with stone structures on top of the platform to make them look even higher!

CENTRAL PLAZA

PLAZAS

◇◇◇◇◇◇◇◇◇◇◇◇◇◇◇◇◇◇◇

The most important buildings in a Mayan city were around the sides of the main plazas, the paved open spaces where people gathered for religious events and other ceremonies.

PALACES

Mayan rulers lived in grand palaces near the center of their city. There would be rooms for the large royal family to live in, space for the families of other powerful people, and rooms for the people who did the work of running the city, so a palace was not really a private home. The palaces were highly decorated, with carvings and bright murals everywhere.

PALENQUE PALACE

BALL COURT

BALL COURTS

The great cultures of Mexico and Central America played ball games both for fun and as religious events. The court usually had a goal at each end, a hard surface for bouncing a rubber ball, and seats on the long sides of the court so people could watch the game. A large city could have several ball courts.

TOMBS

◇◇◇◇◇◇◇◇

Underneath the great buildings of a Mayan city would be the tombs of its great families. Sometimes, a tomb for a family rising to power would be built on top of an older building!

Quiahuiztlan

BUILDING MATERIALS

◇◇◇◇◇◇◇◇◇◇◇◇◇◇◇◇◇◇◇◇◇◇◇◇◇

The Mayans lacked a lot of the building resources that we think of as essential: carts with wheels to carry heavy loads, animals like horses to pull the carts, roads for the carts to move along, metal tools for cutting both wood and stone, and pulleys to help in lifting and positioning heavy blocks of stone. What the Mayans did have was a lot of people, and almost all of their great buildings seem to have involved a lot of muscle-power and not much else.

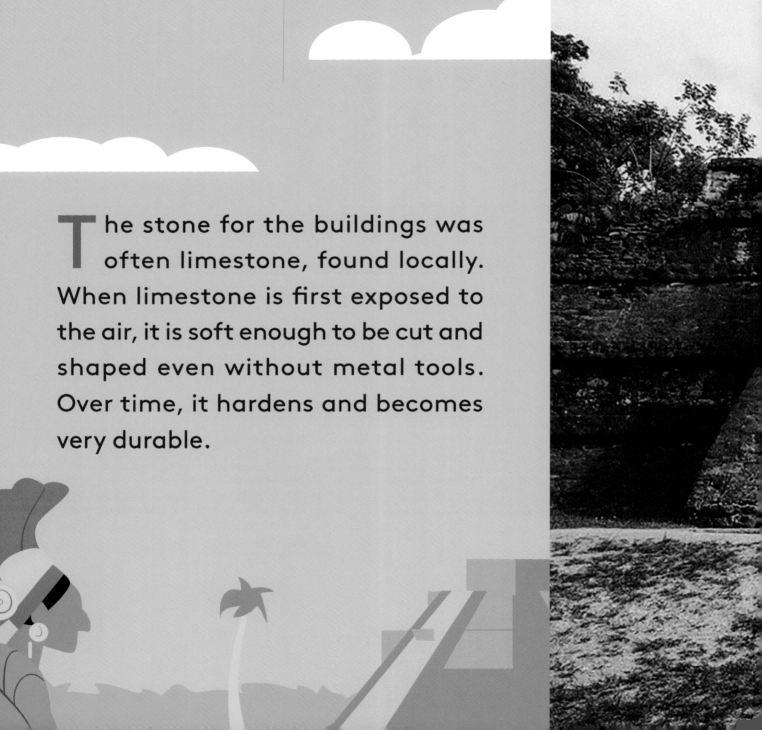

The stone for the buildings was often limestone, found locally. When limestone is first exposed to the air, it is soft enough to be cut and shaped even without metal tools. Over time, it hardens and becomes very durable.

Private houses, as opposed to great buildings like temples or palaces, were often made of wood with adobe (dried earth) walls and thatched roofs. As you can imagine, a lot of these more modest buildings have disappeared over the centuries.

THE CULTURES OF THE AMERICAS

Across North, Central, and South America, millions of people formed hundreds of cultures that lasted thousands of years. Learn about some of them in Baby Professor books like Getting to Know the Great Native American Tribes, Aztec Technology and Art, and The History of the Inca Empire.

Visit

BABY PROFESSOR
EDUCATION KIDS

www.BabyProfessorBooks.com

to download Free Baby Professor eBooks
and view our catalog of new and exciting
Children's Books

40183214R00040

Printed in Poland
by Amazon Fulfillment
Poland Sp. z o.o., Wrocław